rockabyebye

Sabrina Youn

BookLeaf
Publishing

India | USA | UK

Presentation by *BookLeaf Publishing*

Web: www.bookleafpub.com

E-mail: info@bookleafpub.com

ISBN: 9789363305427

First edition 2024

For the one who was always there, and still is.
Even now.

Omma.

back in the beginning

Hold my hand and lead me back to
a smaller world and body

I'll visit my books and dolls and bed
You'll bury me seven feet deep

Scattered eggshells made of steel
bleed out tiny soles
I don't mind the pricks so long
as I can keep my dreams

insomniac

desperation is fragrant
huddling under blanket forts
a shield of surveillance from my god

like a wounded animal, I lay on my side
allowed to suffer and wait

breathe,
          breathe shallow,
breathe quiet and quick

limbs stay still, stay dead
I'll close my eyes
retreat to my head
and ignore that he can see me

writer's fever (poetic edition)

worse than stuffy noses and sticky coughs
is an illness i wholeheartedly embrace
it strikes the muse dead every midnight
and continues long thereafter

symptoms include a fiery pit embedded in one's gut
antsy fingers and knocking knees and a carnal want to write

i flail for relief when afflicted
torturously enticing
rolling words in my mouth again and again
till it's set in stone and i
collapse

further

My family moved 14 times before
Settling in this small apartment
Wherein lies my first memory
a choice freely given

I was, what, 7? When Omma asked
"Which room do you want?"
She was puzzled when I picked the tinier one
Really? Are you sure??
Well, no, not really now that you ask that
But you and Appa are bigger and I am not
Was I supposed to be entitled to more?
Was I meant to grow?

Sometimes I would regret it later
Realizing, not that I could have more, but that I *should*
    should,
        should,
           should what?

I debate, but don't give me choices.
Familiarity sides with punishment.

ensalada

할머니's recipe

> cut lettuce (dash of vinegar to clean)
> 1 tomato
> quarter of an onion (my sister hates this)
> 1 freshly squeezed lemon (my sister loves this)
> 4 spoons of extra virgin olive oil
> spoonful of salt
> a whole lot of sesame seeds and sweet corn
      i left and never came back
      will i ever see this land that borne me?
      must i belong anywhere?
> mix well

selfless sympathy

to walk mountains in many shoes,
not just mine own,
is our best form of travel

i wear the too-small shoes of a confused child
pink bows and scuffed sequins
then the too-large sneakers of an aging, hurt man
rubber worn out from running and running

dusty sandals from the desert
gem encrusted heels
leather boots with bite marks
socks drenched in blood

they don't always fit, and sometimes it hurts
but i'll always keep trying

for our interlingua
        wishing you could touch
        my words

eat my thoughts

                and digest the   dissonance

seatbelts

The happiest I've ever been
was the day after my church retreat
I felt so spiritually strong; I'd for sure get into heaven
Tasting no fear, of eternal torture, the gnashing of teeth
That ride home I was freed,
praying to die right then
A willful exit was prohibited
but maybe an accident
    maybe a car accident

    maybe that's why i still have trouble putting my
seatbelt on

The American Nightmare

My parents sought the dream
Flew after it when I could barely walk
We cut off my Spanish / Korean tongues
and I was baptized

They wished on a helicopter star every night,
for an elevator, escalator, stairway even
So when a hand offered a ladder, prophetic
they climbed

Climbed while carrying me tight to their breast
Climbed through rearing my sister
Splinters be damned they climbed and climbed till the very
same hand
pushed them off

and we fell for miles

And I might've heard something crack
And still we lie here, concrete jungle, watching the stars
wink out
I woke, stayed woke from such visions and yet I tell myself

it's just a bad dream

bibimbap

> rice
> kimchi (cut up, pour in juices)
> meat (patty, 갈비, any leftovers... egg?)
> add sesame oil and seeds
> add 김 (i also like 매운 멸치) and gochujang
it does hurt that all i have are broken phrases
melodies ages old
blood even older
> mix well

sapient

Have you ever seen another species study other species
merely out of curiosity or fun?
Have you ever seen another species kill so fanatically
torture themselves and animals alike?
Have you ever seen another species so kind, sympathetic
that they took in and cared for other species
just because they wanted to
just because?

for the greater the potential
the greater the tragedy

I'm so scared of us
And I love us too

memory glass

I am who I am
ever changing, ever constant
a floating mind on a drifting planet

At times I am jolted
when reminded of what I am
(a passing comment
glimpse of a mirror)
My sex, my ethnicity, the like

I then recall that it's important
but believe me when i say
at the moment, most moments
I forgot myself

I acted as my actor
ever changing, ever constant
a falling body on a mound of others

# of course

i've never seen her cry so much
into the kitchen sink
jerkily washing dishes as her face leaks over

i knew before she said it

so that night i cower and cradle
a hard blue screen in a soft cave
i can't scream so i hiss
i look and look and look and look and-
[BEG BEG BEG] GOD GOD GOD!!!
-and all i get is

'Stage IV,
        metastasis,
                unlikely,

~~i'm sorry.~~'

message 490

God left me on read
and i tried
but i couldn't cry

what is left

No because that's bullshit. FUCKING BULLSHIT. Omma always told me, how god only takes people once they finish serving his will—this great plan only he knows. Their time is up and up they go, except, that's just plain wrong, because Omma had PLENTY more to tend to here on Earth: my highschool graduation and acceptance to UCLA and our first cat and my published stories and films then my college graduation and just literally every milestone possible, she needed to teach me how to drive to share more recipes more stories, I wanted to see her continue being my best friend and mellow out and drink our first shot together and maybe realize that she deserved better, that she had other options, that all I EVER wanted to do is give back a home for her and keep her comfortable and free and happy and

well

now i don't
      i just
now…

…what the fuck do i work towards?
(travel?) *No, I can't leave.*
(writing?) *I was always going to do that anyway.*
(art-) *THERE'S NOTHING*
      there's nothing

there's nothing left for me but Nothing

chicken milanesa

> slice chicken breast
> ready bowl of seasoning (salt and pepper, oregano, chili powder) and egg
> stab chicken into seasoning then punch into breadcrumbs
> cook with ample oil
> serve with rice and ensalada and gochujang
> eat
> close eyes
> feel at home
> feel not alone

return nabiya

no one is given the chance to feel themselves
rise out of which they were borne
would it not be cruelty to let me
feel myself go back?

OR
was it that we already had, well and fought,
clawed gnashed ripped towards fruition
Then forgotten our metamorphosis
to protect the butterfly's mind?

to possess myself

mierda
just let me keep me
to any worldly being of power and sway!
i could kneel, scream, kill for the option

the choice—to die—when i wish

selfish and impossible i know
but none else brings me comfort
to the point that i miss being brainwashed
i don't give a shit if i become stardust
if i reincarnate to the cycle of life or whatever—
bitch! Make me immortal!!

when i can afford to not be tortured
the Nothing scares me most
to never be or think again
my eternal internal, gone and dead

no No NO no

my luminescence leads not to
the cosmos nor Creator
and by everything holylike do I want to **live!**
please, anyone, PLEASE LET ME EXIST AND LIVE!!!

gochujang

> 2:1 ratio of gochujang:doenjang
> add some vinegar
> a spoonful of sugar
> this is genuinely *mandatory* in my life
> where i live is wholly dependent on its availability
> on gochujang geography
> hahahahaha
> mix well

double negative

One form of nothing weighs down my gut
Hooked on with heavy chains
It's sharp and sore, stomach split open,
spilling too much to carry

The other form of nothing frees me
Lungs light from numbing gas
It's heady and boring, strays my mind
to an empty prism with colors, no light
(it's nice)
   (i prefer it)

Coward that I am
too frightened of Nothing to join it, not ever,
not typically
I'd have to be in Hell
for each unforeseeable second
an unforeseeable fate
   (ignore heaven)

But come new dawn I discovered
If these two nothings unite, my every
waking
moment
becomes just that

    HELL

My mind wailing to feel something more
than the confines of nada, of hollow frenzy
My gut, resolute in nullness, as the heart above
shrieks

all things do pass
but i'm still left to clean
what mess i've made of myself

games and all

sprint across rippling trees
or disappear deep within
to my worlds and tree vein timelines
       of ancient regrets turned gold
       of tragedies and triumph
       of blood and pain and gore
       [oddly comforting, to suffer]

other times I would pretend
to be a character gone

happily gone in bone and soul
a monotonous checklist of tasks
until all is said and done
(it might be wrong, but i don't care)

keep wandering

if my heart lies content in company
my ribs sing
for my friends who keep me busy
          made me unashamed to be
for my friends who understand
          raised by my neck of the woods
above all my baby sister
          who fused with said heart
          who i'll never forsake
and for my family who carried me
          even when it hurt them
          even when it hurt me

i've known for a while it's not about gods or magic
but people
it's what you make your whole world
in a universe this cold and beyond
it's about learning and caring
in that exact order

and if I could thank anyone
I would thank you